Mind Your Head UK

Awareness, Stress & Confidence

By

BARRY TAPLIN

Published by Mind Your Head UK

United Kingdom

www.MindYourHeadUK.com

First Edition

ISBN 978-0-9556935-0-2

About

Barry Taplin MAC

Barry is a member of the Association for Coaching and is a full time life coach.

Barry was born in the UK and still lives in a leafy Sussex village in England with his wife Val. Barry & Val have been married for 35 years so a good couple to gain the experience needed for a truly great relationship and ask yourselves how that can happen in this day & age? They have 2 sons.

The experience Barry has accumulated over the years *(some details below)* is as vast as it is broad which has enabled him to see all aspects of how people run their lives and **COULD** easily improve if the desire is there.

Management Experience

Barry has over 30 years of management / consultancy experience.

Barry is a certified Senior Management Interviewer for a leading UK company and has interviewed many hundreds of people ranging from young folk just out of school looking for their first job to senior management roles in corporate business & government in and outside the UK.

General Election

Barry stood in the United Kingdom General Election and was rated in the top 6 of 550 achievers in his particular area within that UK General Election.

Business Owner

Barry has been the Director & Owner of three businesses and understands the issues that small business owners go through. Next in the Mind Your Head UK series of books will be on the subject of people skills and management. To contact Barry go to: **www.MindYourHeadUK.com**

Testimonials

1. "Barry leads through relationship management"
2. "I have found Barry an inspiration"
3. "Barry acts as a career coach by helping people learn and accept their weaknesses and offers methods for people to work on them."
4. "I have always admired his tenacity and willingness to move forward, both in the areas of work but most importantly in peoples' development."
5. "Barry was a big inspiration to me for his constant engagement"
6. "He had a vision and motivation."
7. "Barry has the ability to create an environment based around trust, this allows people to take risks and test their own ability."
8. "Barry is honest, diplomatic and always gives accurate and constructive feedback based on his experience, empathy and understanding of people at all levels he is dealing with."
9. "Barry has the emotional management skills to understand different personality types require different management techniques."
10. "I can rate Barry as one of the best.

Contents
"Awareness, Stress & Confidence"

		Page
Did You Know		7
Chapter One	The Real You	8
	Are You Aware You Are Two People	9
	Evidence That Emotion Over Logic Wins the Game	14
	Who Are You	18
	You Need To Think You Can Fly	22
Chapter Two	The Stress and Worry Cure	28
	Basic Generalisation about Stress, Worry and Anxiety	29
	How Not to Handle Worry	30
	Ways To Knock Down Those Worries	37
	The Three Parts To (or States) to Stress and Worry	41
	CBT Means Cognitive Behaviour Therapy	48
Chapter Three	The Power of Confidence	53
	Assessing Yourself	54
	The Food-Mood Connection	63
	Unlocking Your Confidence	71
	Lets Conquer The World	81

Introduction

You have just made the best investment in your life if you take on board this valuable life enhancing information. I would recommend that each of the three chapters (which are each broken down into 4 x 1 week sections) are best read and worked on in order. You have the rest of your life to live and enjoy so let's do this right once rather than come back at a later date.

You will be rewarded by the information you will take on board. This book is all about the knowledge that you will be able to retain after reading it….. For Life!

The knowledge will be sharp, concise and to the point, easy to understand but above all if you incorporate it within your life at home or at work and genuinely take on board this information you will be one step ahead of others who do not practice these skills.

ENJOY YOUR BEGINNING

Barry Taplin

Did you know the following

How We Discover Information:

81%   Due to seeing with our eyes.

12%   Due to our hearing.

4%   Due to what we smell

2%   Due to what we touch.

1%   Due to what we taste.

How We Hold on to Information:

30%   Due to what we see and read.

60%   Due to what we see, read and discuss with others.

90%   Due to taking an action on what we have read and seen.

The above is the reason I have broken each of the three chapters into four weeks with a small number of tasks to practice each week. The format is specifically written for a reason and although some of the actions may seem simple they will have a positive impact on you and those around if you follow my suggestions.

Remember this information will be beneficial for you in many aspects of your life be it at work, with friends or within relationships. Is it magic?. Well no but **as long as pigs have pink ears** people will begin to respect your new found confidence and gravitas.

Let's get some of this "Life Skill" information across to you. Now.!!

Chapter One

The Real You

The Real You

WEEK ONE

Are you aware you are two people?

You are the **rational person** who will view all situations with some form of logic and assess the situation that is placed in front of you. The rational side of you will follow your head as opposed to your heart. This part is the more thoughtful person inside of us where we need to consider the options and make what we think is the correct decisions given the evidence placed in front.

You are also the **emotional person** who follows your heart rather than your head. This part of you is sometimes overwhelming in that you just have to do something that is logically the wrong thing to do. The "emotional you" can be impulsive and sometimes illogical...As an example of this the relationship of a friend of mine fell apart and while he was talking I could see that his eyes were becoming tearful... he was the big I am and stating "Yup all over it now 100%, no problem, need to move on" But really in his heart he had not moved on. He was trying to force the logic to override the heart and I could see through it but he couldn't.

We all know sometimes what we should logically do but we just don't not want to do it do we? Some people call it a gut feeling; this is another way to do what we really want to do in our heart as opposed to what logically we really know we should do.

Our minds are finely balanced with these two little people on each shoulder one called Mr or Ms Rational and one called Mr or Ms Emotional.

Both in fact are good to have around but the time to watch out for is when one begins to take control over the other and your thinking or decision making becomes a little erratic or unbalanced.

Now you are aware that you are two people, which one do you suppose can be the more powerful overriding person? Well it is without question the emotional side of you rather than the logical side.

There are studies that are continuing as I write this where those running these investigations are ascertaining if emotional intelligence (EI) is more important than IQ intelligence. From my opinion and perspective I would say yes, and when one begins to understand the reasoning behind this, in that emotion overrides logic, it can be used in many different areas. Advertising is a good example of where this happens and you will see some adverts that will have a scene that has an emotional *lean* to it, this will make you remember it and far more likely to remember and purchase the product rather than if it came out and simply said "stop me and buy one". My company Mind Your Head UK.com is another example where we believe fun is the key in life. Fun is an important emotion hence our silly movie and happy little song on our web site which gives you a good feeling, and there is nothing wrong in that as happiness is a food of life. Silly is Good!

The more you understand this aspect the more potential you have on controlling your life for the better or even other peoples. Have you ever listened to a boring presentation never to be remembered or have you heard a presentation with a few jokes or a depth of sadness within it... either way you will remember the latter more so than the boring non-emotional one.

One more example is have you ever listened to a piece of music that brought back memories of an emotional time good or bad. I suspect you will remember that far longer than a logical decision you made at exactly the same time no matter how excellent that decision was.

The Real You

WEEK ONE ASSIGNMENTS

So for the whole of next week this is what you need to concentrate on:

When you have to make decisions and remember you will make hundreds of decisions a day without even realising it, but some you will ponder over. Take a note and see whether you made it from a logical aspect or from the heart... also remember there is no right or wrong answer here as either could be the best choice. The point I want to make is that generally something with emotion in it will have far more effect than something that hasn't. Hence IQ is very important but I am believe that EI (Emotional Intelligence) is more important because it has more of an affect and you will retain that incident or information for much longer.

No matter where you are or who you are, be it manager, student, wife, husband or partner this understanding of EI over IQ which you will be aware of but maybe never understood how important it was. It is a key driver on understanding what drives people, business and relationships.

Employers base a lot of their recruitment on qualifications and much less emphasis on an applicant's attitude or what I call the **"Emotional Altitude"** of that person. My belief is that employers need to pay far more attention to that aspect when interviewing. From my experience and I have been a senior management interviewer for a British blue chip company for a number of years, is that the evidence that I have massed totally confirms this policy that few companies follow. Of course qualifications are a guide but we believe that EI is equally important as IQ.

If you are a manager when hiring or interviewing anyone, place as much emphasis on their personal skills and their EI abilities or what I call **"Emotional Altitude"** skills in addition to their schooling qualifications. A full interview process and more information can be found in Life Skill four called **"Secrets of the British Corporate Interview".**   www.MindYourHeadUK.com

If you are in a relationship Remember a logical answer to a special person is not always the best way forward because if you **put your foot in it** (a British saying meaning you have said something you should not have... or wish you had not!!) it may be remembered for a long time to come.. far better to provide an emotional & logical answer with feeling so that your partner believes you understand them.

If you are a student. When you have to address a meeting or go to an interview your qualifications will get you into the door but it will be your character and **"Emotional Altitude"** that the interviewer will remember... give your interview emotional likability. !!!

The Real You
WEEK TWO
Evidence that emotion over logic wins the game.

Horace Walpole, 4th Earl of Orford 1717 -1797 author and politician (***The son of Sir Robert Walpole, England's longest ruling Prime Minister***) once said that **"Life is a comedy for those who think and a tragedy for those who feel."**

As this quote shows the understanding and evidence comes thick and fast throughout the ages that emotional intelligence is as important as IQ and as I have mentioned at the start of this chapter, I would advocate more so than IQ but it has been very rarely recognised as a skill or ability or indeed an asset at all. The whole ethos of our lives in today's society is based around formal (IQ led) qualification and education.

The emotional mind is in fact far quicker to respond than the rational logical mind. It will spring into action with almost no thought what so ever of the consequences, the emotional mind will do this in a split second, its quickness refuses to listen to the logical mind telling it to hold back on that encounter and take stock of the situation before we act...... The reason this happens is that it goes back to the inbred reactions of our ancestors (as mentioned in Life Skill two "The Stress and Worry Cure".). We had to be vigilant 24 x 7 x 365 because if we weren't it could cost us our lives. Just a split second error on our ancestors' part could mean being attacked and eaten by a wild animal. Just think about it, a wild beast is in front of you and you are wondering "do I eat it or does it eat me" !... nope you just do not have that time. Your reaction will immediately spring into action without proper reasoning.

There are many examples of where instant reaction has caused an incident to happen whereby the person that took that action looks back and wished that they had not responded in such a way.

As an example of this, in the UK (and I suspect the rest of the world) "road rage" is being encountered on a more regular basis and on an odd occasion people have been killed due to the emotional actions of one of the drivers.

There is no logical thought but pure emotion to get back at that driver that cut you up on the main road of freeway. Afterwards of course and in most cases there is deep regret as the reasoning is so absolutely futile to be ridiculous a reason to pick a fight or argument with someone. Can you imagine those people that spend years of their lives locked away in prison due to a moments emotional folly !!

The Real You

WEEK TWO ASSIGNMENTS

So for the whole of next week this is what you need to concentrate on:

This week is all about forgiving... yup that's what I said, forgiving, as now you understand that when people get angry (and that may include yourselves) quite often it is the inbred immediate reaction to something that has come through 50,000 generations or more.

If you find someone acts in an inappropriate manner without a second thought, the chances are they will feel really bad about that an hour or two later. There are those of course that enjoy inflicting problems on people but they are more premeditated, what I am talking about here is an action that is so swift it catches you by surprise. THAT is the illogical emotional mind of the individual taking over. By not responding aggressively and allowing them to think about their actions they will realise that they acted the wrong way. If you simply argue with them they will simply argue back regardless.

This one is not easy as you need to control your emotional mind more than they do but now you are aware that you are 2 people you can take steps that will give you far more control and ultimately respect from everyone. There is nothing so gracious than not arguing.

If you are a manager understand that all people have different personalities. There are many tests that are available to ascertain what type of person someone is. Attempt to find out more about your staff or indeed your bosses personality make up. Once you have you will be able to deal with both your staff and your boss in a way that doesn't emotionally impact them to a degree that **upsets the apple cart** so to speak !!

If you are in a relationship and you have an argument... (we all do from time to time and some more than others) try and back off and see if it is a direct emotional response or a much more premeditated response, either way arguing is always unproductive so why not show your other half a far more controlled uplifting person that has the ability to choose to argue... Or NOT !!

If you are a student you will understand that some young people can get out of control so quickly and you need to decide whether to take no notice or start the conflict that they are keen to progess. Well !! you know what the answer is and if you are concerned of looking silly in front of them.. Well "Big Deal" you have more important things to do than waste your time in conflict rather than having fun... remember ....**Life is Just a Bowl of Cherries!!** Every moment in our lives is precious so do not waste time in any unnecessary conflicts.

The Real You

WEEK THREE

Who Are You

Psychologists use the word "metacogntive". See more on "CBT" Cognitive Behaviour Therapy in Chapter Two **"The Stress and Worry Cure"**. As a term that refers to awareness and process of how we think. The word that is used to mean the awareness and process of one's emotions is called "metamood". These are terms that are used by psychoanalysts regarding discovering ourselves or self awareness. What we are really talking about here is being very observant about what we are doing in this very moment in time.

"Mindfulness" is another word and if you surf the net you will discover just how this too can teach you to be observant in the present rather than continually look into the past or the future.   When we really begin to concentrate on the here and now, we observe ourselves and our surroundings in a way that we have not done for such a long time as we always tend to take everything for granted.

Here is a good example which I will also ask you to do in week three skills. Next time you eat a bar of chocolate or enjoy your favourite sandwich or light snack concentrate on that alone... Look at it and feel the texture and see the colour, savour each bite and feel what the texture is like, the taste and finally the swallowing of it... quite often this simple act takes you by surprise as you never knew how pleasant the item that you were eating or drinking could be!

This one very simple test will also allow you to understand just how little we think about not only our everyday actions but also about ourselves... we simply plod through life talking to others without any real self awareness or self observation. Those last two phrases mean that you are aware of your mood and thoughts; it is only once we are aware of these that we can improve or change.

Self Improvement may not just be about gaining an extra qualification; it can also mean that when you are in a bad mood that you become aware of it and work towards improving that mood. It is all about recognising this moment in time because we nearly all just drift through life on automatic pilot.

Another example is for those that drive, how often have you driven to work or college and wondered how you got there? You had to drive and change the gears but you really do not remember doing it... you were on automatic pilot and lost that time of observation forever!!

This week is about how to be aware and find out from within yourself what it is you need to improve or change? If you can find out and observe yourself you will have started the journey of self improvement.

The Real You

WEEK THREE ASSIGNMENTS

So for the whole of next week this is what you need to concentrate on:

For one hour each day observe (this does not have to be one hour in one go, you can break it down into groups of minutes.)

- Be aware of as much as possible in that hour

- Be aware of how you drive,

- How you eat,

- Even how you clean your teeth,

- In fact anything you do can be observed more than you would normally do.

If you are a manager When you are in a meeting this week view everyone in detail. Look at his tie and shirt.. is that a strange combination or what !! ☺ Look at her dress .. wow is that colour the right colour to be wearing ? View them in detail but also be aware of how you are feeling sitting in the meeting, are you nervous?.. if so deep breath as no one will know! Learn more about this in Chapter Two **"The Stress and Worry Cure"**.

<u>If you are in a relationship</u> View your partner in more detail than you usually would... you may get some strange comments from them if you are noticed... "What are you looking at me like that for?" You may see them in a light that you had not noticed them before... Remember this is just an exercise on observation and not to make any assumptions about them but just to observe in a way you had not done for such a long time?

<u>If you are a Student</u> Look at your tutor and study their details... just to yourself.. not just their looks and clothes but also their mannerisms, had you realised that they kept scratching the back of their head for example...

This is all about being aware of others and yourself at this moment in time and you will discover just how much detail you are missing every day. This is just a piece of the jigsaw where you will begin to discover the real you.

The Real You

WEEK FOUR

You need to think you can fly

Have you ever noticed that when someone has a problem or a failure quite often they will lay the blame on **<u>fate.</u>** When they are successful they tend to credit that success on **<u>luck</u>**. !

If you have a negative attitude your thinking will be: "I will believe it when I see it" yet those with a positive outlook will constantly believe it without seeing it. They will just strive ahead regardless of any facts that may get in the way.

I'll tell you a little story about a friend of mine which to me sums up just how a good positive attitude can fool people into success........ even themselves !! I played the game of squash for 18 years, I played 4 or 5 times a week for all of those years, I coached people in squash at a reasonable club level. I even entered some county wide tournaments. I was never a World Champion at Squash but I wasn't so bad!.. Then one day I asked my friend who became a Managing Director of one of the UK's largest blue chip companies (turning over £billions) if he wanted a game of squash, he said yes but also said he had never played that game before.

Well he was a good friend and I thought it would be good to show him how to start off and he may take the game up as a hobby. My friend, by the way is the sort of person who oozes confidence and gives you the impression that he is an expert in everything. I had respected that confidence for over 20 years. We both arrived on the squash court and at first he could not hit the ball, after 15 minutes we were having a bat and ball game. What happened next I will always remember and from that game and incident I learned the power of confidence. After playing for 40 minutes I suddenly found myself listening to him tell ME where I was going wrong!! It was as if I had been hypnotised into believing that he was the best squash player in England.

He really believed in himself to such a degree that for a few minutes I believed him as well. It was truly a strange experience but proved that a sheer positive attitude can have some truly amazing effects on others. To this day I have not reminded him of that incident but I learned a great deal from that hour of squash back in the 1980's and about how the positive mind can truly work and convince others.

..... I am sure something like this has happened to you at sometime or even you may know someone who seems to be an expert in everything and no doubt they are quite successful!!

A positive mind links in very closely with the information given in the first week and that is the power of emotion and belief.

Your life will progress in the direction of your most foremost thoughts as no one can make you fail except yourself. This week is not about the "how" to think positive, it is about you understanding the power of positive thoughts and that they DO actually work. There have been numerous books written on positive attitude, dreams and goal setting mostly from the USA and there is now chapter three of this book and it's an English version!! called **"The Power of Confidence"**. It could change your life. ?

The Real You

WEEK FOUR ASSIGNMENTS

So for the whole of next week this is what you need to concentrate on:

Before you rush to the shops to buy the first "Positive Thinking" or "How to Create a Good Attitude" book you can see that you need to convince yourself as much as you can that they actually work otherwise you will read the first chapter and then leave it, as long **as pigs have pink ears** I bet that will happen. So make a list of the people that you know that seem to ooze confidence.. Now analyse them..

- Are they successful?   (I Think...... Yes)
- Do they really know as much as they think they know?   (I Think... Not)
- Do other people that know Mr or Ms Confidence believe that they know the answer to most things? (I Think... Yes)

- Are they extravert? (This one may sound obvious but I say not always. YOU can be a very successful introvert as long as you have that confidence, so if you are shy you too can be a great success.)

One thing I must make VERY clear and that is make sure you know the difference between the individual with natural confidence and the guy or girl that is just a "Know it all". The simple way to tell is if they are likeable or not.... Pure confidence you will like, A "know it all" you will be wary of.

If you are a manager You are in a great position in that you will have quite a few egos in your company to do this analysis on.. ☺ Also bear in mind what you are looking for is confidence within a person and then ascertaining how successful they are and even how successful they will be in the future. Very rarely are negative thinking people successful. If they are they would have reached that position when they were positive. !!

If you are in a relationship there is nothing better to come home to or meet up to a positive person is there?. There is a Life Skill on the Mind Your Head UK web site in the series **"How to Influence and Manage People at Work or at Home"** which tells you how to adapt certain people skills towards others in greater detail and this links in very nicely to having or portraying a great attitude towards your partner. Be positive, they will love you for it. Try not to say one negative thing all week about anything or anyone...

If you are a student you need to differentiate between youth and over exuberance which most young people have... some still have that when they are 70 !!. What you are looking for is a positive attitude that shines through and the respect you have for that person. They may already have had some success? They may be a chairperson of some committee. Equally you can analyse a person who you know is at the top of their profession... are they confident and positive? (I think yes they would be)

You may find that some senior figures may have your respect and the respect of others but if you can get to talk to these people you may find that they don't know as much as you thought they did... they are just very confident.. Politicians are always good to analyse in this manner no matter what Country they are from... go and see your local politician. !! and remember I stood in a UK General Election and soon learned that the persona of the person that is portrayed is not always the same as what is within... you can **never tell a book by its cover** is an on English saying which is so true. To learn more on how to adapt check out chapter three **"The Power of Confidence"**

Chapter Two

The Stress

&

Worry Cure

Present fears are less than horrible imaginings.

- Shakespeare -

Basic Generalisation about Stress, Worry & Anxiety

There are varying degrees of worry. Imagine you were walking up the stairs on the Eiffel Tower in Paris. Well, there are 1652 steps to the top of this magnificent structure, let us say step one is someone who has zero worry or is anxious in no way whatsoever and step 1652 ... well you don't want to be there!! Well we are all on those steps somewhere and I expect we would all be on a different one as well. I would suspect that there would be no one on the first step.. in fact I would be surprised if anyone was on the first 100. Then we may come across an individual on step 101 that is calm & content with life and are a joy to be with.

Quite often meditation over many years would help you progress to this level (or step 101) which is a feeling of supreme contentment & calm. I would say most of us kick in at about step 300 and this life skill that I am about to go through is aimed at those that hover between step 300 & step 1200 although all levels would take some benefit from the advice. The below information will help all those (the large majority) on whatever step but professional help may be required is some cases.

Therapies such as CBT "Cognitive Behaviour Therapy" works wonders and I will touch on that in this chapter.

The Stress & Worry Cure

WEEK ONE

How NOT to handle worry

Let's start off in week one on the things that most worriers have heard all before:

- Stop worrying, everything will be OK.

- Be more positive.

- Everything will be OK in the end.

- Take your mind off it.

- Get out more.

- No point in worrying, as my Grandma used to say.

Quite often this advice from well meaning friends is ok and can work but sometimes it can have the reverse affect... Try being positive NOW!! You will immediately home in on your anxiety and it may increase slightly.

Have you ever tried being as anxious as possible deliberately.. if you do you will probably find that your anxiety levels begin to drop. Worry is a strange phenomenon in that in most cases it is just ourselves telling us the wrong thing. Anxiety is generally worrying about things that were in the past or things that may happen in the future. Anxiety is not as a rule about this moment in time. Worry and anxiety is based on the old adage of fight or flight.

What is fight or flight?.... well it goes back a long time....a very long time, when our ancestors were living in caves and the main aim in life was not about what to buy at the supermarket or how will I pay that bill or even how will I ever find a husband or wife... no the only thing on the mind of a Neanderthal was survival...it was 100% inbred.

Survival was the name of the game for thousands and thousands of years.....over 50,000 generations have had fight or flight built into their makeup. Over a period of a very long time things can really become inbred.. for example it has been discovered that certain species of fish that live in extreme depths of the sea are totally blind due to living in a world of total darkness and therefore not requiring the use of sight.. over a period of thousands of years they have evolved to suit their environment. Equally the fight and flight survival strategy of our ancestors exists in today's human traits.

When we become worried some senses in our bodies change in number of ways such as sweating / palpitations / tensing of the muscles and so on.

Example:

Your boss wants a report on his desk by 09:00 in the morning and it is 17:30 and you're just off home! For a worrier panic sets in and you think "Oh no I'll never get that done" and your levels of anxiety begin to increase. Heavy stress, by the way is adrenaline that pumps into the body.. it just takes 7 minutes for that adrenaline to dissipate.. so you see, you DON'T have to be anxious forever!! Just 7 minutes ☺

Let's continue on how not to handle stress and one of those ways is to avoid creating what are called safety behaviours. Safety behaviours are actions we put in place "just in case" we panic or need help, it is a way in which we feel we can control situations.

For example, because one of the affects of anxiety can be the feeling of breathlessness you may begin to avoid exercise because you associate breathlessness with anxiety. Thus the safety behaviour here is not to exercise as you believe it creates anxiety.

Another example is the fear of getting anxious when you go out. In this situation you carry some form of medication such as a sedative just in case... but what you are doing is simply reinforcing the belief that an anxiety situation may occur.

If we worry about something and avoid it or put in place some form of safety behaviour we are in effect giving a legitimate reason for us to worry about it. We are reinforcing our beliefs that the problem is so bad that we need to worry about it.

Let's take another little example.. you may not like spiders. If spiders really stressed you out, you would find yourself looking for them and only go to places where you think you can avoid them.. by doing this you would gradually promote a phobia in yourself about spiders.. it would just reinforce your belief that they are horrible creatures even if you do not come across any.

Most of us would never get to that state but you understand the idea of how a simple thing, no matter how small or silly, can get out of control for some people and it is all down to the way you think. Far better to pick the spider up and move on.

Not easy I know but after the initial uncomfortable feeling you would subconsciously know that there was nothing to worry about and eventually you would pick a spider up as **you would pick a daisy.**

Solving worry is very much about confronting our worst fears, once confronted it gets easier the next time around but if we don't confront them we reinforce those fears.

One of modern day's biggest fears is speaking in public or doing a presentation in a meeting at work or college. Never easy but the longer you delay the confrontation of this fear, the worst your fears will become.

Here is a little suggestion that **_WILL_** help. Do the presentation in front of a family member or close friend who is prepared to film it.. if possible a few family members or friends just to up the uncomfortable level a bit. Treat the presentation seriously from start to end... so get the silly laughing and feeling foolish out the way at the beginning. Now before you look at the recording think of how you felt on the "Richter" scale of anxiety before you did the presentation.

I expect you would be about 6 or 7 out of 10... possibly higher.. in a real presentation you may feel you were 8, 9 or even 10 (I know I used to think that). OK now look at the recording, my bet is that you appear to look on a level of no more than 2 or 3... You see others DO NOT see how you feel... That is a very important confidence boosting piece of analogy that you need to remember!

The Stress and Worry Cure

WEEK ONE ASSIGNMENTS

So for the whole of next week this is what you need to concentrate on:

The first thing to practice this week is to find something you just don't like to do and that makes you a little anxious and I am not talking about standing to be the next President or Prime Minister of your Country.. no I am talking about something very simple and about a level 3 or 4 on the anxiety level. Let's say you don't like to call your boss or answer the telephone when you know it is him or her calling.. well you know what I am going to say don't you... make a point of finding excuses to do this on a regular basis.. At least twice a day everyday for the next seven days.

Make a list of things that worry you or make you feel anxious and put those in order with 1 being the least worry and so on, the list can be as short or as long as you like but in this first week we are just concentrating on the lower worries. Let's say you have 12 things you worry about, well just work on the 4 that worry you the least... easy easy is our motto as we gradually gain more confidence and worry less...........

Make no mistake **as long as pigs have pink ears** we *ALL* have anxiety and <u>**YOU**</u> need to understand that we are all the same in that respect.

Now begin to work on these areas as I have mentioned with the example of the boss and the telephone. Maybe you don't like to socialise as you feel embarrassed and nervous.... so you know what.. go out with a group at lunch time or in the evening... you need to keep doing this until the levels of anxiety gradually subside and it becomes just a level 1 anxiety which is quite natural in our daily lives. Once those areas of anxiety subside still continue to do them from time to time so that you continually keep those intensities to an acceptable level.

So now you have the first tool in your bag to help with life's daily anxieties. Simple but effective but more than that, it keeps those anxieties from becoming so big that they dominate your life in a way that restricts your life.. you have things to do, people to see and life to get on with.. it's an exciting place out there. ! so let's get some control into it... Are you game? If so do it.

<u>**If you are a manager**</u> I know at times you will have projects to do with very little time and with deadlines so ridiculous that it all seems so impossible. But as the old adage says on how do you eat an elephant... answer.... a bite at a time which is so true.. you can only do so much. But in this week we are talking about the smaller concerns and worries where we will begin to home your senses into the right direction. !

<u>**If you are in a relationship**</u> and you find yourself in an anxious situation.... If your partner arranges a social event that you feel uncomfortable about such as meeting some of your partner's work

colleagues or friends who you have never met, suggest that you meet with one or two of them at a time until you feel happy to mix with a group...once again you are confronting your fear but on a small manageable scale. Make a point this week to meet one or more of them.

If you are a student (and this is just an example but you may have a more relevant worry) generally many students would not have come into contact with seniority to that much of a degree. Head Tutor / Bank Manager even your local MP. Make a point this week to make contact and keep building on this week by week. Even your local MP will have what they call surgeries at a place near you where you can go and ask their help or suggest something like a better local bus service... and if you feel uncomfortable and think it would be an idea to give it a miss then that's the one to do !! Go for it.

The Stress and Worry Cure

WEEK TWO

Ways to knock down those worries

This week is all about the logic of worry and attempting to get some perspective on the situation and put things in the right context.

Let's move on from last week's smaller worries to the bigger issues in your lives. Bear in mind the methods that works well for the smaller worries also work well for the larger ones and visa versa.

So what is it that is worrying you.... the first thing to do is write it down. Simply in doing this can bring the issue more into the open and helps you confront the problem. It is all too easy to just put your worries to the back of your mind where they just begin to fester. So get all the facts down on paper in order that you know what you are dealing with.. look at it as rational as you can and you may see through that hazy mist of worry and anxiety and find that actually it is not as big a problem as you thought...

If it is as big as you thought, you need to mark a score at the side of the worry. Most things people worry about never actually happen... so if your biggest worry is turning **into a pig with pink ears..** mark the likelihood down beside it on a scale of 1 to 10 with 1 being not very likely and 10 being it really could happen... in my view that particular worry would have to be a zero !!

At each step we are beginning to very slightly diminish the possibility of the worry actually happening for real.

So let's say you have written or evaluated it from 1 to 10. Now let's think what is the worst that can happen and think would it really happen.. To some people where stress gets a little too overwhelming it is called catastrophic thinking... This means they keep seeing the worst in each situation and it spirals out of control: for example someone may think "If I don't get this project out, I'll lose my job then have no money and lose my house then my family"....... of course in reality this infrequently happens and it is just your silly old mind doing overtime, but at the time this thinking is VERY REAL indeed to the individual who is thinking it ....isn't it!?

Generally by this point you may see that your worry is not as big as you thought. If it is why not check out what I call the cost-benefit breakdown. By this I mean put yourself in someone else's shoes and pretend to get them to check your issue out for you. Ask yourself "will keeping this thought actually help me solve it or not?"

Why not do as I have said... gain all the facts, and then do your best to make a decision, (sometimes just making a decision be it right or wrong can be a very big relief) and move on. Even wrong decisions can have benefits as every successful person invariable makes the wrong decisions where of course they learn by their mistakes and the next time they make a better decision.

The Stress and Worry Cure

WEEK TWO ASSIGNMENTS

So for the whole of next week this is what you need to concentrate on:

Write your problem down with as much detail as possible.. I don't mean write a book but get as much fact down as possible.

Now analyse it and give it a mark from 1 to 10 to see if it was as bad as you thought.

Now pretend to be someone else looking at your worry.. is it really worth the worry.. will that worst thing really happen.. I would suggest it won't.

At the end of the day one has to make a decision about the worry and move on. If you wanted to produce a 20 page document for your boss but could only make it 15 pages... finish it and move on as the fact that it was 5 pages short will be forgotten by the end of the week.

If you are a manager you need to evaluate your workload and NOT waste unnecessary time on crossing every "T" and dotting every "I".. The 80% / 20% rule is always a good rule... 80% of the document will be accomplished in the first 20% of the time. Why spend another 80% of your valuable time completing just 20% of the document. Bear in mind what we are talking about here is a stressful situation and when you are in a state of anxiety this rule is a good one, as why put yourself under further pressure.. Sure if you want to create a 100% document and you have the time without stress 100% isn't a bad number to aim for is it !!

If you are in a relationship and you have financial worries or your partner just won't discuss the problem that is making you pull your hair out, you could work it through a third party to get the issue moving. Confidentially try and discuss the issues with a good friend of your partner and ask them to suggest a discussion as a way forward to deal with the issue. As my Mum still says brushing anything under the carpet does nobody any good in the long term.

If you are a student as an example you may be worrying about your course work or exams but if you follow some of the skills above they may not eradicate worry to zero but they will help, and together with the other weeks information it will help to diminish the anxiety and get the whole thing in proper perspective. After all you could win the lotto or lottery next week.. maybe not but bad things have a habit of becoming rather good after a while..

The Stress and Worry Cure

WEEK THREE

The Three Parts (or states) to Stress and Anxiety!

Well what a surprise, just when you thought there was only one.. The one where you find yourself so anxious and worried that you can't seem to control yourself.. so you think, but of course you can.. This week I'll tell you the three things that creates the uncomfortable state that you and I call worry, the state that makes you feel oh so bad... and tell you a trick or two to help. The information here may not be vast in words but it will be as important as all the other words put together so take note !

State One – The Body

OK number one of three that creates (and is a part of) anxiety is the reaction of worry on your body. You get anxious and the first thing that happens is your body is preparing itself for the "fight or flight" situation. Here is an example of some of those symptoms which may happen:

- Your heart beat may increase
- Your hands may begin to sweat
- You may start to tremble
- You may get palpitations
- You may find you cannot sleep so well
- Your stomach may begin to churn.

State Two - Behaviours

Next in line is our actual behaviours and how this can actually have an effect on whether the worry dissipates or carries on. This is mainly what you do when faced with a worry that begins to get a little overwhelming. You may just want to run away from the situation.. You may have heard of people having panic attacks which are as about as uncomfortable a body sensation as you would want but is rarely harmful and this sensation will flow away again after a very short period, as little 15 to 30 minutes. This behaviour, together with other actions such as avoidance can reinforce our anxious beliefs.

State Three – The Mind

This is the thinking state "How we think about a situation" and how on earth can so many of us get this so wrong so much of the time... because we ALL do !! We see and picture certain beliefs in our mind and begin to believe them. It is so surprising how our thinking can affect us and move us into the wrong direction. Surely we all have control on what we think, don't we ? Well the simple answer to that is "Yes" we do have control but it takes effort to control something and that goes for the mind as well. I have often advocated to anyone that cares to listen that to have a good life you need to eat well and exercise our bodies to keep our muscles strong and toned. What many forget is to exercise the mind as well on a daily basis. You have come across positive thinking books and wondered do they really work.? Well of course there are many forms of positive and good attitude books. I have read many and in most cases felt great afterwards, that has to be better than watching the very depressing news every day.

So there we are, the three areas that "Is" Anxiety. Anxiety can reduce confidence and self esteem, it can be a vicious circle that spirals down unless we can add some "good feeling" in our minds along the way to keep the balance and harmony in ourselves to an acceptable level.

The Stress and Worry Cure

WEEK THREE ASSIGNMENTS

So for the whole of next week this is what you need to concentrate on. I am going to tell you how to help yourself deal with those three states.

State One – The Body

There are many ways of convincing the body and ultimately the mind into a state of well being rather than being uncomfortably anxious. Breathing exercises have a big impact on this state because when you are anxious you generally shallow breath... this week when you worry make sure you breathe deeply! by this I mean breathe from the base of your stomach rather than shallow breath from your chest. The good thing about this is you can do it anywhere and no one knows that you are concentrating on this aspect to bring your body to a calmer place.

So breathe in gradually through your nose to the count of 3 and then taking twice as long to breathe out through the mouth counting to 6 as you do it. This is fooling your silly mind and body into thinking that you are calm and that there is no fight or flight action to take... this is just one of the tools to help with worry.

If you want to take this further there are many books on breathing as well as classes such as Yoga and Tai Chi that concentrate and help on how to breathe properly, all of which will help enormously.

State Two - Behaviour

A lot of behaviour issues are around avoidance. You may remember my story in the first week about picking up spiders if you are frightened of them and the more you put it off the stronger the association becomes and the worse the fear becomes. Presentations are a fear for many of us but actually what is really the worst thing that can happen?.... you forget your words and feel a fool but most people around you wouldn't even be aware that you lost your way... so do it !! This week pick one or two things that you would normally avoid and do them... as often as possible.

If you find it hard try and break down the avoidance into steps and build up. As a simple example (and you could relate this to your specific avoidance) if you find it hard to shop at your local supermarket... begin just to go into the supermarket and out again without buying anything, then the next time buy one item and the next more shopping until you feel comfortable to do a whole weeks worth in one go. These steps can be over a period which is comfortable to you.

State Three – The Mind

Your thinking is critical to get right and you need to keep adding good thoughts rather than bad. Imagine in front of you there are some weighing scales with some chick peas on both sides, one side is negativity and the other side is positivity, generally the scales balance and hover in the middle when life is chugging ... when you are worried what happens is you begin to give yourself these negative thoughts which tip the scales on the negative side... too many chick peas on the wrong side...

You need to add some chick peas on the other side to get that balance back again. You need to evaluate the situation as I mentioned in week two and get back on track. There are lots of ways to help here such as going to the local gym or cinema, maybe going out for a meal with your loved one.. basically what we are talking about is whatever is enjoyable to <u>YOU</u> are the positive chick peas that we all need all of the time but especially when you are feeling worried.

It is not easy to motivate yourself if you are stressed or depressed but it is at these times you need to push yourself to enjoy yourself.. even if it is pretending to enjoy yourself it will be the first steps to ***REALLY*** enjoying yourself.

If you are a manager

1. Breathe properly - this is invaluable in stressful meetings or situations.
2. Try _not_ to avoid the things that make you worried.. (Within reason!)
3. Enjoy some good things in your life and add those chick peas to the positive side of your life scales

If you are in a relationship

1. Breathe properly.
2. Try _not_ to avoid the things that make you worried.. (Within reason!)
3. Enjoy some good things in your life and add those chick peas to the positive side of your life scales

If you are a student

1. Breathe properly.
2. Try _not_ to avoid the things that make you worried.. (Within reason!)
3. Enjoy some good things in your life and add those chick peas to the positive side of your life scales.

You will notice that this week the above practices are the same for all people... a life skill for life.

The Stress and Worry Cure
WEEK FOUR
CBT means Cognitive Behaviour Therapy.

I mentioned these three words in week one under the paragraph called "Basic generalisation about Stress, Worry & Anxiety for this course". I will now go a little deeper into this subject with some helpful tips that will help you to get through life. To begin with **Cognitive** means "thoughts" and **Behaviour Therapy** is what it says.

Therefore if cognitive means "thoughts" then CBT therapy which is practiced throughout the world is all about addressing the biases in your thinking that creates those worries and anxieties. (Or even depression which I have not touched on in this life skill.) CBT therapists will help you to evaluate your thinking and help you understand what is called "Error Thinking" as well as "Core Beliefs" that are set at the back of your mind and which you may consciously have not even been aware of.

This subject is a book in its own right and in this final section I will give you some ideas on the first stages of CBT and how it can help in everyday life.

It is always best to identify your worry just as we have done in week two by writing it down as there are actually productive worries as well. These are there to help us and can be a good thing but there is also the unproductive worry – this is the area that the worrier needs to address.

You need to challenge that "error thinking" that is the trigger for much unnecessary worry such as "I may fail at my job / I may make a fool of myself if I go to the party / I am sure I will mess that presentation up / I will fail in my exams and my friends & family will think I am useless". As you have already learned, most of these incidents will never ever happen.

For some reason you will focus on some things but not others. How come you worry about some silly things but not some of the major things that others worry about? This could be a core belief that is at the back of your mind which you may not yet be consciously aware of. You may need to trace back step by step why you are worried about a certain thing. Here is an example:

Let's say you feel that you always want to give 100% and really worry if you don't.. you may be thinking you are a failure but then why do some people just accept the fact that 80% is good enough and move on. It could be that as a child you had parents that demanded 100% otherwise you will grow up to be a "nobody". Many parents do this with all the best intentions. This is just an example that those words said with best intensions by many parents may have placed a belief in the back of your mind that if you don't achieve 100% you are a "nobody"..

Even now you are 10 or 20 or even 40 years older that seed is still in your mind. Until you can be aware that it is there, confront it, realise they were doing what they thought best and then eradicate it as some error thinking, it will continue to raise its head from time to time.

Bringing things out into the open can be an emotional roller coaster but if you don't it will be there in the background forever. For some you may need the support of a therapist to go through this with you.

The Stress and Worry Cure

WEEK FOUR ASSIGNMENTS

So for the whole of next week this is what you need to concentrate on:

Let's now go for the number one worry in your life, the one worry that gives you so many sleepless nights or costs you so much of your time in thinking about it. This may not be a big issue to some but it is to YOU!. It makes no different what the subject matter is, it is just your biggest worry no matter how small or big it may seem. This subject has the biggest impact on your worry scale. Identify and write it down.

Now you have identified your number one worry you need to ascertain whether it is a rational worry or if it is your mind not looking or analysing it in the correct way. This term is all about "Challenging Dysfunctional Assumptions".

To give an example you may think that in the future you may lose your job or your family but what you are doing is distorting your thinking to assume the worst, you could equally assume the best couldn't you ??.

Another classic example is you think someone doesn't like you... But you really don't know so you are assuming the worst once again.

There are so many bad assumptions and in all of those situations you could equally assume the best couldn't you ? Therefore every time you assume the worst... also assume the best ! ...but assume the best more times than you assume the worse... does that make sense? Let me explain that for every negative thought you need to add at least 3 or 4 positive thoughts to balance out your mind. Speak to yourself in a positive manner on a number of occasions.

This may sound silly and it does not happen overnight **but as long as pigs have pink ears** it <u>**WILL**</u> help you.

Finally let us attempt to go back in time and try to ascertain a time when this huge worry of yours first started. Try and link this current overwhelming worry into something that happened in the past and that just maybe you are still clinging onto. Most of these incidents would not have been deliberate but they do just happen and these incidents can affect us for a long time and in some cases can grow in strength as many phobias do unless we attempt to find that core belief where this worry stems from.

Once again there are many good books and organisation that will help with CBT if you feel that is the need.

<u>If you are a manager</u> your valuable time and time management would be an important factor but equally the situations that stress you out at work could well be based on other outside influences.. try and spend some time on the above three paragraphs in week 4 to ascertain if there are deeper reasons why you get more anxious at work than you feel you should. But equally remember that we do all get worried and anxious. Worry can be a good thing as well as a "good" warning.

If you are in a relationship and you are worried (as an example) that your partner may leave you, try and see through the haze and mist of worry and gauge if this is really correct thinking. Go through the above paragraphs and you may just find it is your incorrect thinking.

If you are a student and you are worried about meeting people or you feel anxious about your exams try and put things into perspective by going through week 4 again. As my saying goes **Life is just a bowl of cherries** and there will always be problems, but there will always be great times as well.

MIND YOUR HEAD UK

Chapter Three

The Power

of

Confidence

The Power of Confidence

WEEK ONE

Assessing Yourself.

With confidence comes the open door of freedom and opportunities. Many of us simply do not have that confidence to do what we would really like to. In nearly every case I have come across, the individual invariably always regrets what they **DID NOT DO** in their lives, more so than the things they did do, even though there were some big mistakes along the way.

Remember that we all mostly regret the things **we didn't do** rather than the things and actions that we did do.! So why is that?

Of course there are acceptations but if I were to ask you to write down a list of items you regret... the majority would be the things you **did not do**. The job you never applied for / the girl or boy, man or woman you were too shy to talk to and gain a date / the idea you had in a meeting but didn't want to look the fool... only to find someone else suggested it and received the gratitude of the senior person in charge when it could and should have been you / the presentation you would like to give but are too afraid of messing it up--- you think you may panic or just forget you words and look a fool / the party you would have liked to have gone to but were too apprehensive about meeting with strangers.

So how unconfident are you? Apart from those indicators that I have just mentioned here are some other thoughts on your confident levels that you may identify within yourself:

1) You do not feel in control of your life.
2) You are always on the defensive and never forging ahead.
3) Your breathing is erratic.
4) You have no targets, goals or sense of direction.
5) You are unsure if you can cope with a forthcoming situation.
6) You take yourself too seriously.
7) You're just not sure about the future.

Confidence then is a feeling within you. How that feeling got to the level it has to make you think that you have no confidence is another issue. **"The Stress and Worry Cure"** in chapter two has more in-depth information on behaviour therapy.

You must feel that you would like more confidence otherwise you would not be reading this. Let me firstly say congratulations in seeking advice as many do not and of course what happens is that their level of confidence either stays as is, or it can gradually worsen unless actions are put in place to reverse that thinking.

This Life Skill gives you the tools needed to turn yourself into that super-confident person you so desire... you have a life to get on with.....you have people to see, places to go and things to do..

Confidence is also a very subjective topic, not only would we rank each other on a different scale than what we think we are on, but in addition it would also depend on the frame of mind we are in at that moment in time.

As an example Friday afternoon just before the weekend your confidence will probably be higher than a Monday morning at ten minutes past nine! So what has changed... your thinking that is all?

You have just conducted that presentation that most people worry about and feel on top of the world because you did it... but 10 minutes before you gave it you were a quivering wreck.. so what happened to make your confidence rise so dramatically?

How would you pick out a super confident person (in your view?) Would they swagger down the corridor at work in a John Wayne fashion? Would they just talk very loudly? It is never easy to pick out that confident person as many introverts are also very confident and as a rule you would just pick out the extroverts wouldn't you.

The point I am making is that you may feel unconfident but you may also just be putting too much pressure on yourself in assuming you can't cope with anything without feeling anxious and uncomfortable. But be aware that everyone ....but everyone, worries about certain situations, therefore do not set your expectations so high that they are unachievable.. Confidence and worry are interlinked and by dealing with one will help the other.

Let me say now that you are a whole lot more confident than you think you are compared to those who may look 100% confident but invariable are not. In my skill on Mind Your Head UK.com "Life Skill four" **"The Secrets of the British Corporate Interview"** I gave an example of how to convince yourself that you are not as half as bad to others than you think you are to yourself! Soon to be out in book two of the Mind Your Head UK series on Life Skills.

So, begin to build those thoughts in yourself in knowing that we are all on the confidence scale at a different level depending on a number of factors that I have already mentioned.

Give yourself some slack and give yourself a treat for:

1) Purchasing the information in this book, you have made a start.

2) Realise that you **ARE** a much more confident person than you think you are.

3) Begin to appreciate that you're not alone as we all lack confidence in different situations and at different times. What is required are some tools and knowledge on how to handle situations when we are lacking confidence and to be able to build on them to become that super confident person.

Of course this isn't going to happen by the end of the week... These skills are not called <u>LIFE</u> Skills for no reason, they are for <u>LIFE</u> and take time to adapt and in this case your confidence will take time to gradually increase but you are now on that road... Remember the phrase on **how you would eat an elephant**.. and the answer is a bite at a time. This old saying was probably one of the best pieces of advice that I learned many years ago when any pressures hit / when any new subject came along that I needed to understand in depth / when I needed to meet an impossible deadline.

Well you and I can only do so much, but you do need to take that first step. When you have taken the first step take the second not thinking about the third and so on.... before you know it you will have completed 30% 40% or more of the task without realising it.

If you jump in feet first the chances are you will come unstuck in one way or another. A step at a time or a bite at a time is the way to gain confidence. !

As I said earlier, confidence is a very subjective subject and is almost all about perception... How you see yourself and how others see you can be both at different end of the spectrum, but you are that same person. Those people that you "Think" are very confident are probably good at acting!!

The Power of Confidence

WEEK ONE ASSIGNMENTS

So for the whole of next week this is what you need to concentrate on:

The point I have put across to you in this first week is all about this:

"You're not half as unconfident as you think you are". !

So let us get that one set in stone in the recesses of your conscious mind and begin to set that into your subconscious as well. To help do this you need to not only read the information above, especially the parts that relate to you, but you need to begin to visualise a time that will soon be upon you when you would like to be that super confident person. Gaining some time alone would be helpful to fully concentrate on this week's skills learning.

Now don't reject this for one minute in thinking this stuff is loopy!! This REALLY works if you work at it. Visualisation REALLY works!! Got that! Many books have been written about this subject of visualisation and the reason is because they are mostly right.

Think of yourself in that situation that is coming up where you need to be very confident... and begin to see it in your mind's eye. See the room, chairs, door, window, desk etc. If the unconfident issue coming up happens to be skydiving then see the plane, pilot, seats etc.. Whatever it is see it and visualise it. Picture it and see it.

Now... Begin to visualise the things that you WANT to happen. See them as they happen all the way through your thinking process from start to finish. This is a discipline that can have dramatic effects if treated with the respect it deserves **as long as pigs have pink ears** please do this as it will increase you confidence.

Do this as many times as you can over the week <u>and every day</u>. 10 minutes here and 10 minutes there or even a full 30 minutes all at once if you can spare the time. I have know some of my readers to do this early in the morning before they go to work while everyone else is still asleep. Do you think they are buzzing on their way to work... You bet they are. ☺

If you are a manager assess where you are on the confidence ladder from 1 to 10 and ask yourself if some of the other managers you think are oozing with confidence may just be bluffing a tiny bit? Are they acting in any way? Let me answer that one for you.... yes of course they are (View the "About" page on Mind Your Head UK.com and you will see I have also seen those guys and girl managers who act most of the time as well!!).

So, you can now climb up a couple of rungs on that confidence ladder now you know that you may not be quite as unconfident as you thought as most of the others are only acting anyway!

If you are in a relationship and you feel that the confidence has been knocked out of you for one reason or another, now is the time to turn the tide and visualise a far more confident you in the situation that you have always worried or been concerned about.

This week is not about actions it is about visualising those actions and seeing you as the person you want to be and handling every situation in a perfectly confident manner.

If you are a student you may be unconfident as you have not been involved in some situations that you are about to come into contact with. It may be an interview, it may be a meeting with someone in authority, the subject matter could be many things. This is the week for visualisation and not actions... see as much as you can in detail about the situation that you would like to be totally confident in and work your way through that situation with the outcome being the one you wanted.

Visualisation is a very powerful tool in gaining confidence as well as being a powerful motivation tool.

- **Visualise your success**
- **Visualise your success**
- **Visualise your success**

The Power of Confidence
WEEK TWO
Mood-Food Connection.

This week is about a subject that may surprise you, in that it can have a big impact on your confidence, general mood well being and that is what we eat and drink. Building confidence is about gaining a number of tools to forge ahead. You can liken it to creating a painting or a picture.

Each part of a painting or picture doesn't mean much if you were just to see a square inch, but if you begin to put all of those small pieces together you get a Rembrandt!! And that is what you are doing at the present,.. you are gathering a number of tools and creating that super confident you... you are creating your own Rembrandt picture within yourself. !!

Did you know that some chemicals in our brains called neurotransmitters are at the front of the queue when it comes to regulating our moods which in turn regulates our confidence?

Some neurotransmitters such as serotonin and gamma aminobutyric acid (GABA) help to calm us done.

Then on the other side of the coin there are others such as dopamine that have the affect of stimulating us into action. What helps to alter the chemical makeup of our bodies is the intake... what we eat.

There are nearly 40 million Americans that have some sort of anxiety disorder which includes lack of Confidence and lack of Self Esteem. Could this have anything to do with food? Could a change of diet really help with mood swings and confidence?

Have you ever felt tired and sleepy after lunch? Well you are not alone as the majority of people feel this way because your blood-sugar levels, which rise after you have eaten, suppress a chemical called orexin, this is a brain chemical responsible for being alert. Hence you're tired after lunch. On the other hand, if you are hungry and your blood-sugar level is low your mood can change to become impatient and even a little angry.

This goes back to our ancestors when they had to be aggressive to hunt if they wanted to survive. We have quite a lot to blame on our 50,000 year old ancestors! ☺ Some information about our ancestors and the fight & flight reaction is mentioned in Chapter Two **"The Stress and Worry Cure"**.

There is a lot more on how we handle our confidence in connection to what we eat than meets the eye. But of course the food-mood connection and our blood-sugar levels are only a small part of the much bigger picture.

Our bodies and our minds simple react much better with fresh, whole foods that provide the protein, vitamins, minerals and omega-3 fats. The reason this is as about as obvious as **pigs with pink ears** is that what we eat affects our production of the neurotransmitters that I mentioned earlier as well as our hormones, our energy levels and the quality of our synaptic connections. All of these factors determine how well we respond to the stresses and demands of daily living which in turn has a major impact on our confidence.

There are mountains of other reasons why you should eat well but this week is my attempt to just discuss and convince you that the food-mood connection is a very real one and together with the other three weeks will benefit you in helping you get to that super confident person.

Below are some facts about the chemicals in your brain. These will affect your confidence and that I hope by understanding these you will change your diet to a better one for a number of reasons that will be of great benefit to you now and the rest of your life...

Eating correctly is a Life Skill!.

- **Serotonin:**

This is a neurotransmitter that keeps your mood firing on all 4 cylinders and keeps you feeling good and helps to keep you confident. It is made from tryptophan, an essential amino acid abundant in fish, eggs, chicken turkey. Iron, Zinc and vitamin B3, B6 and C help to convert other chemicals to serotonin.

- **GABA:**

This also helps you to stay focused and calm which in turn helps with confidence. GABA is found in halibut, legumes, brown rice and spinach. Vitamin B3, B6 as well as B12 will help to convert other chemicals to GABA.

- **Dopamine**:

    This chemical is responsible for the many "Highs" that you feel. The brain converts the amino acid tyrosine which can be found in protein to produce dopamine. Extra tyrosine can be found in almonds, avocados, dairy products, pumpkin and sesame seeds. A related compound called tyramine is rich in aged cheeses, such as aged Stilton and other aged cheeses.

So by now you may begin to think that there just may be something in this food-mood subject that I have been writing about this week and could it really affect your confidence...

<u>OF COURSE IT CAN AND IT WILL !</u>

Well if I am beginning to turn you towards a better diet I have done my job... if you are still not convinced please look in the book shops for food-mood books and convince yourself further as this really is yet another part of that Rembrandt picture we are creating for you.

On the next page is a table that I hope you will adapt and work towards. All of these symptoms will have a large impact on your confidence, begin to knock these down or eliminate and your confidence will also improve.

The GOOD "Mood Food" Table

Symptom	What is good	Try and Avoid
Anxiety	Almond, apple, apricot, aubergine, basil, bean, beetroot, celery, lettuce, peach and pulses.	Caffeine
Depression	Oats, walnuts, fresh fruit and veg, and B vitamins.	Alcohol and Caffeine
Headaches	Almonds, basil, broad beans, cabbage, camomile, cherries, chive, fennel, ginger, mint, oily fish, onion, peach, white meat.	Alcohol and caffeine.. try drinking drinks that contain, apple, camomile, mint or apricot.
Insomnia	Aubergine, basil, barley, camomile, corn, courgette, lettuce, onion, pumpkin. A carbohydrate snack before bedtime	Well well !! Caffeine again !
Mental Fatigue	Fruit and veg, apricots, shellfish, food with vitamin B, zinc and selenium, basil, mint	... and again... ! Alcohol and Caffeine

With anything that I suggest you will also need to make sure that you are not allergic in anyway and if in doubt check with your physician as this is a generally based information skill that is to act as a guide only.

The Power of Confidence

WEEK TWO ASSIGNMENTS

So, for the whole of next week this is what you need to concentrate on:

I could have written this week as a book in its own right but the objective was just to plant the seeds and understanding within you that gaining a better dietary regime for yourself can have many benefits in many areas...

Building your confidence is just one area that you will benefit from if you follow this week through and keep evaluating and changing your diet for the better.

This week please create your own menu. Create a daily menu (Morning / Lunch and Evening) for each day... so you need to create seven of these. Once you have completed one week, create a second week.

Now I would not expect you to change your life's eating habits in one week, but I would like you to create what you believe is the perfect diet.... you may have to do a little research on this or even pop out and buy an inexpensive book on how to eat. Look for Mood-Food books.

If you are a manager.

If you are in a relationship.

If you are a student.

This week everyone is in the same boat in that once you have created your dietary menu you will need to work towards implementing it at home / at work or at uni or college.

Now DO NOT change it all on day one, a Monday as by Thursday you will be so desperate for some fast food that you will feel you will have failed and give up. I would rather this take you three months to last you a life time rather than 3 weeks to last a month... so like all my Life Skills implement it slowly and comfortably so that you enjoy the experience.

Make no mistake eating the correct food will have a positive impact on your confidence....(as well as a number of other areas)

The Power of Confidence

WEEK THREE

Unlocking Your Confidence.

Do you know what a "NAT" is......?

No, it's not an annoying little fly. It's actually short for Negative Automatic Thoughts. N.A.T's are the most basic form of thinking that you need to begin to reverse. These unwanted N.A.T.'s fill our heads with unwanted thoughts without us even realising it.. Until now that is!

These thoughts affect our moods and our confidence on a daily basis and flow in like a spring tide through our minds on a regular basis without us even knowing.

They have a number of characteristics.

- They are automatic in that they just pop into our heads.
- They are distorted in that they are not factual but are exaggerated.
- They are telling yourself lies! You accept these N.A.T.'s as real facts and because they are mostly part of your subconscious you don't even question them.
- They come as they wish and you can't turn them off.

Yes that's true...! You can't turn them off..... But once you know that they exist you can look out for those N.A.T.'s and begin to eradicate the negative with positive.

Imagine if you were to teach a baby from the moment it was born that the grass was the colour red and not green. It would always believe that the grass was red... It would not even question the fact. It would only be when the baby began to understand, talk and listen that it would learn the truth, even then it would still need someone or something to make it realise that all of those years it was wrong.

At first it just would never accept that the colour of grass was green but as it gained evidence and the truth from a number of areas the penny would drop.. ! But unless the question was posed it would never even think about investigating it... as that is how it is... the grass is red.

Now what I am telling you is that the grass is green. ☺

I will set you a task this week to begin to home in on these N.A.T.'s and show you a way of how to reverse the thinking as these really do have a big impact on your confidence... this will be another tool in creating that Rembrandt picture of yourself!

If you can find out and observe yourself you will have started the journey of self improvement.

Controlling Your Fears.

Lacking in confidence is linked closely with all of our other thinking processes in that nine cases out of ten it is our distorted and incorrect "Error Thinking". Nowadays we worry about paying a bill or a meeting with someone that can knock our confidence.

Back in the 18th century one of the biggest fears was being certified as dead when you were actually still alive, that is why coffins had a bell so that it enabled the supposedly dead person to ring and let others know that they were actually alive! Thank goodness we don't have those worries any longer. Managing any fears affectively will of course also hugely build your confidence.

Phobias as example can be created through incidents that may be totally unexpected. As an example when a friend of mine called Christine was walking to work one day she stumbled over a broken paving slab and hurt her leg badly... she was off sick for six weeks and when she was ready to go back to her job she insisted that her husband took her by car as she was fearful and frightened that she would fall again...

Christine's confidence in walking to work had taken a severe knock in just one incident. I am sure you can think of many incidents that may have happened to you where your confidence has taken a battering. Once you know how to manage your fears, your confidence will build accordingly.

Confidence is all about managing our fears!

This next tool may seem simple.... but it works! and that is the very effortless art of breathing properly, especially in times of anxiety or floundering confidence.

Below is a repeat sentence from Chapter Two **"The Stress and Worry Cure"** because it is <u>**SO**</u> important ....which will help you on how to breathe properly in those times.

>>>>>>

There are many ways of convincing the body and ultimately the mind into a state of well being rather than being uncomfortably anxious or unconfident. Breathing exercises have a big impact on this state because when you are anxious you generally shallow breath... If you feel unconfident in any situation make sure you breathe deeply! By this I mean breathe from the base of your stomach rather than shallow breath from your chest.

The good thing about this is you can do it anywhere and no one knows that you are concentrating on this aspect to bring your body to a calmer place. So breathe in gradually through your nose to the count of 3 and then taking twice as long to breathe out through the mouth counting to 6 as you do it.

This is fooling your silly mind and body into thinking that you are calm and in turn is another tool to build your confidence.. If you want to take this further there are many books on breathing as well as classes such as Yoga and Tai Chi that concentrate and help on how to breathe properly, all of which will help enormously.

>>>>>>

To truly be confident in picking a spider up you need to pick it up on a regular basis.

- To truly be confident in public speaking you need to speak in public on a regular basis.

- To truly be confident when dealing with people in authority you need to deal with people in authority on a regular basis.

- To truly be confident with meeting people you need to meet people on a regular basis

- To truly be confident in interviews you need to have an interview on a regular basis.

Do you notice a theme running through the above points... and the list could have been 100 other worries that you may have. We all have them, myself included and we all lack confidence to a different level on different areas.

What you need to understand is this: Do not put pressure on yourself by assuming you can be 100% confident with everything... that just is never going to happen with anyone on earth!

If you need to be confident within certain areas then begin to practice within just those areas. Why try and be 100% confident with sky diving if you're never going to sky dive... my confidence level would probably just about reach one!

My analogy on this is as follows:

You can learn and be confident 100% on one thing. You could if you wanted be confident and learn about two things... that would equate to 50% confidence on each... if you were confident and learnt about ten things that would be 10% each... if you tried being confident on 100 different things in life the chances are you won't be confident in anything....

You see there are different levels of confidence depending on how many areas you want to be confident in. You really are more confident than you think.!

The point I am making here is, do not expect to be super confident in everything.... NO ONE is!!

So.....to become confident we need to face our fears and work through them one by one in the areas we want to concentrate on. We need to understand where we lack the confidence and transform those fears into confidence through the actions given within this life skill.

One last point on this week and that is that you may not think so but you will be confident to some degree in a number of areas... why don't you write a list to prove this... you may just be surprised if you really spend some time on this task.

The Power of Confidence

WEEK FOUR ASSIGNMENTS

So for the whole of next week this is what you need to concentrate on:

N.A.T.'s

With regard to the N.A.T's its time you began to identify them. In just knowing that they are there is a huge step forward, as you can then begin to truly understand them and eradicate them.

This week is a four stage process on N.A.T.'s that will help your confidence.

1) When you have to accomplish a task and you go a bit wobberly as the unconfident part of you kicks in try and ascertain what it is you are thinking about. What was the trigger, what were you thinking about?

2) Now think about what went through your mind.. Were you afraid of giving that presentation or going to that interview or even applying for that interview.....even meeting up with someone? It could be anything that blots your confidence. What went through your mind.. Write it down.

3) OK, you have now ascertained the trigger and think you know what went through your mind and you have written it down. What would be the consequences if that did happen? Don't try and think logically for just a moment, but simple write what you think your mind is telling you. These N.A.T's by the way can get out of control so that in some cases you can think some awful things... But you're not alone!! What do you think would be the consequences no matter how bad?

4) Now is the time to take a deep breath and review and dispute these facts that you have accumulated... You need to analyse each of these thoughts and ask yourself are they really realistic thoughts or not... I would say that 98% of these N.A.T.'s are totally unhelpful and create what is called "Error Thinking" which in turn will knock your confidence.

The four stage anti-unconfident process.

1) What was the trigger?
2) What were your beliefs?
3) What do you think will be the consequences
4) Dispute those consequences.

Breathing

Begin to concentrate on the very simple breathing exercise that I mentioned when or if you begin to wobble a bit in certain situations... it really does work!

Confidence

You're never going to be 100% confident in everything. Write a list of the areas that you are confident in.... you may just surprise yourself.

If you are a manager. Whatever it is where you feel you may lack confidence in you need to begin to address those areas otherwise that particular hurdle will simply get higher as time goes by... yes it is uncomfortable but like all my skills, my suggestion is to implement a stage at a time... how do you eat an elephant... a bite at a time...

Break the situation down into steps and attempt to do a step at a time on a regular basis and remember this is not a race... it's a Life Skill... if it takes three months so be it.

If you are in a relationship. Maybe you feel you just don't have the confidence to bring up a subject that you want to discuss with your other half. Well, what you need to do is write this subject down in detail, get everything you want to discuss down on paper and then break it down into steps wherever possible. Try and approach the issue a stage at a time.. and as I said this is not a race... it's a Life Skill. Therefore do this in your own time... but do it! and set timeframe to it, no matter how long..

BUT keep to it.

If you are a Student and you feel you lack confidence in certain areas such as... being interviewed is one common lack of confidence, meeting with people in authority is another, or just going out to a function in an evening and worrying about who you will meet and making a fool of yourself.

Well do the thing that you feel most uncomfortable about. Make a commitment to do one of those things this coming week... now do not worry, I remember doing this years ago and to begin with I hated it... that was giving a presentation.. was I lacking in confidence or what !! in the end I did it more and more and ended up standing in a General Election talking to hundreds of people at political meetings.. a challenge I thought I would never have achieved.. But I did, and I did it at a step at a time.. as I suggest you do.

As I have said in the other two paragraphs above.. this is not a race but a Life Skill. Do it but at a step at a time. Good Luck let me know how you get on.

Well this Life skill is quite a varied one but it is important that you do all of these actions, some of which may not sit right such as your diet but believe me the impact would be dramatic!

Let's move on to the last week....

The Power of Confidence

WEEK FOUR

Let's Conquer The World.

Here are some of my thoughts on how to help improve your confidence.

- No matter how bad things get, it is YOU that can chose on how to react. No one else in this world can ever take control of your reaction.. So choose to react positively.. it is your choice and no one else's.

- Say "Yes" more than "no" as "Yes" means focussing on the positive. Positive = Confidence

- Trust yourself and trust your instincts.. You are as good as the actors out there! So don't be fooled.

- There are no wrong decisions in life; I have found out that I have learned so much from all the bad ones I have made.

British philosopher Francis Bacon 1561 – 1626 said:

"Truth emerges more readily from error than from confusion"

British Prime Minister Benjamin Disraeli 1804 – 1881 said:

"Great services are not cancelled by one act or by one single error"

- Feel the fear and do it anyway.... you will feel on cloud nine afterwards.

- An error doesn't become a mistake until you refuse to correct it.

- Always visualise the best outcome... it's a great habit to get into.

- Create your own positive affirmations and repeat on a regular daily basis..... forever, as practice makes perfect.

- Thinking positive is great, writing positive is even greater and doing positive is greater than the two of those put together.

- Always look on the bright side of life. (A song by Eric Idle from the 1979 film Monty Pythons Life of Brian.) sing it every day

- **Life is Just a Bowl of Cherries** as you will see all over the Mind Your Head UK web site.

To become confident you also need to be assertive.. you need to be a person with gravitas that others respect. Coaches like myself, believe that the assertive skill set is as valuable as any other in business and in life.

Used and learned properly it can boost and promote your self-esteem as well as have other effects such as lower your stress levels and of course increase your confidence.

Those of you who know assertive people will find that they are generally liked and respected, they are not afraid of saying "No" diplomatically. They value others as equally as themselves; they have principles and will stand up for what they think is right.

Whether you agree with their beliefs is a different matter but you will respect their point of view.

Assertive people take responsibility for their own actions and are not afraid to make mistakes or ask for help. They also express themselves openly with others and can handle conflicts when it may arise.

These are the traits that you now need to begin to learn ....a bite at a time! **Over your Life!.**

Have you ever been somewhere where you were just desperate to make your point? It may have been a meeting of some sort where you truly believed you had an excellent point to make but were too shy, too self-conscious, and too unconfident to say it. ? You just never piped up and afterwards wish you could turn the clocks back... well you are not alone, we have all done it. To overcome this and begin to forge ahead next time it happens (I expect this will happen in one way or another every week of your life) simply breathe properly as I have described, relax and make your point in full confidence.

Say your piece and sit back in total command.... I know....I know your stomach will be churning and your head will be spinning but you did it!! Act out the total assertive person... if you act enough times it will become part of your makeup. From now on **PRETEND** to be confident!

There is no magic pill to put right incorrect thinking; you have to work at it until it is ingrained in your subconscious and as I said in week two you WILL finally see that the grass is green **as long as pigs have pink ears** that will happen.

Changes in Your Life

It maybe changes that have happened in your life where you may feel that your confidence takes a bit of a dive and needs to increase. Understanding why this happens will help.

Well, once again you really are not alone in this area as there is a predictable pattern where your mind takes you if any changes are made in your life. These changes can be planned are unplanned and can relate to almost any aspect in our life.

If we know what to expect when changes happen at your work place, home or college it will make you far more confident in knowing that we all feel the same.

Here is the roller coaster of your

Emotions and confidence to any changes.

Stage One: **Astonishment & Refutation.** The first thing that happens is that you are a little taken back and shocked as well as wanting to deny the change or you may even trivialise it in some way and try and laugh it off as it will never work.. What are they thinking of? Performance and motivation: This is on a reasonable level at this stage but begins to drop.

Stage Two: **Confrontation and Apprehension.** This stage is where you will begin to lose confidence and worry about the new circumstances that are about to happen or have already happened. You may find the new changes hard to take in or agree to and your emotions may become stronger as well as having feelings of being fed up.

Performance and motivation: Both are now rock bottom and your confidence is at its lowest ebb.

Stage Three: <u>Experimentation.</u> Now you know it's for real you begin to dip your toes in to see how cold the water is. Your activity will now increase as you begin to test and examine the new changes.

Performance and motivation: Both are now on the way up to and you are becoming more confident as you take in the changes.

Stage Four: <u>Commitment.</u> By stage four you have taken on board the changes, you realise that putting up any resistance is futile in the long run. Your confidence is now on a high.... possible even higher than before as you have now accepted the changes. You are now working with the new changes.

Performance and motivation: This is now at a level higher than when you started or heard about the changes. This whole process can take any amount of time as the changes are implemented from weeks to months.

The Power of Confidence

WEEK FOUR ASSIGNMENTS

So, for the whole of next week this is what you need to concentrate on:

- Begin to be more assertive. You don't have to be abrupt to any answers you may give but simply give the answer YOU want rather than the answer you think the person wants to hear. Learn to say no..

- Write down four affirmations and repeat then daily at different times of the day.

- Learn to be an actor.. This one will not only have instant impact but you will begin to change your habits for the better until this is ingrained in your daily actions. (I did say there was no magic pill that would improve your confidence straightaway, but by acting you can make others think you have taken that magic pill and of course ultimately you will be that super confident person that you are acting out)

- You now understand how most of us will react to change. (unless that is we are the implementers of the change) therefore accept that four stage process with confidence.

If you are a manager You will be aware that there are changes made on a monthly basis within your place of work. Of course they are not necessarily all good changes either, as the top guys and girls need to be seen to be doing something even if it is reinventing the wheel again like so many of them do... In the corporate world the implementation of change goes in circles.. as the saying goes what goes around comes around..

Why waste a moment of your precious time and emotional effort (and not forgetting those sleepless nights)... Just understand it WILL happen in the work place until the day you retire so accept change happens both good and bad and understand that four stage process... Don't become unconfident as that process happens to us all.

If you are in a relationship don't say yes to everything if it's really not what you want. Of course there is always a balance here in that sometimes as an example, if you really do not want to meet up with your partners colleagues but equally if it does mean the earth to them..... in this case I would always say do it.....

But there is a balance to be struck and if you decide to make some radical changes can I suggest that you implement them gradually... remember always in Mind Your Head UK.com we eat elephants a bite at a time... We actually love elephants by the way!!

If you are a student it can be critical to say "No" to certain things. You will know what is right and what is wrong and just because your friends do certain things doesn't mean you do. Be assertive, stand up for yourself and say no if you don't want to participate in a certain things.. sure someone may laugh due to their insecurity but what they will have is more respect for you.

After reading this life skill the biggest thing I want to put across to you is that you are nowhere near as unconfident as you think you are. What you are doing is looking at others and basing your level of confidence on their acting.! No one can be 100% confident in everything so be the best you can, take on board all I have said and keep working at the visualisation and affirmations of you being a super confident human being after all **Life is Just a Bowl of Cherries.**

Well I hope you enjoyed the book and have learnt some skills that you will hold with you for the rest of your life.

Mind Your Head UK.com is a British instructional site devised by me, Barry, a person that has life experience and information that would be useful for students / relationships or management at any level.

It contained as much information that was necessary and not so much **gobbledygook** (a real English word that means small talk) that you become bored.

Have a great life you only get one!

& Remember

Life is Just a Bowl of Cherries

Barry Taplin

Founder of Mind Your Head UK & Author of this book.

To Contact Barry Go To:

www.MindYourHeadUK.com

The next book in the series of Mind Your Head UK volumes will be about People Skills & Management / Motivation.

www.ingramcontent.com/pod-product-compliance
Lightning Source LLC
Chambersburg PA
CBHW021347090426
42742CB00008B/764